Precious
in His Sight

DEVOTIONS & PRAYERS
FOR KIDS

Precious
in His Sight

DEVOTIONS & PRAYERS
FOR KIDS

Jean
Fischer

BARBOUR **kidz**
A Division of Barbour Publishing

Introduction

Who can keep us away from the love of Christ?
ROMANS 8:35

Jesus loves all the world's children. He wants them to get along with one another, respect one another, and behave in ways that please God. He also wants them to love themselves. *Precious in His Sight* was written for kids just like you. You are special and one of a kind, different from all the rest. But although you are different from every other kid on earth, in many ways all kids are alike. As you read the devotions in this book, you will learn what you and other kids have in common, and you will discover ways to get along with one another. Maybe what you learn will lead to making some new friends.

DEAR JESUS, HELP ME TO UNDERSTAND, ACCEPT, AND LOVE ALL KIDS, WHOEVER THEY ARE, WHATEVER THEY LOOK LIKE, AND WHEREVER THEY LIVE. AMEN.

God Is My Heavenly Father

"Do we not all have one Father?
Has not one God made us?"
MALACHI 2:10

Do you know there is only one God and He made you? He created you and knew you and loved you even before you were born. He planned your whole life. When the time was just right, God sent you to live on earth. He put you into a family and set people all around you to love and help you. Best of all, God promised always to be with you. Although you can't see Him, you can trust He is there. He will never leave you. He will love and guide you all the days of your life.

DEAR HEAVENLY FATHER, THANK YOU FOR CREATING ME AND LOVING ME. THANK YOU FOR PROMISING TO STAY WITH ME AND HELP ME EVERY DAY. AMEN.

I Am Special

We are the clay, and You are our pot maker.
All of us are the work of Your hand.
ISAIAH 64:8

Whenever you draw or make something, it is your own special work of art. There is none other like it because you created it to be one of a kind. That is how God made you. You are one of a kind. God makes each person different from all others. Each one is special and precious in His sight. People don't just look different. They are different in many ways: where they come from, things they are good at, what they like and don't like. Can you think of some ways you are different from your sister, brother, or a friend?

DEAR GOD, THANK YOU FOR MAKING ME SPECIAL
AND UNLIKE ALL THE OTHERS. I'M GLAD I'M
DIFFERENT. DIFFERENT IS GOOD! AMEN.

The World Is the Lord's

*The earth is the Lord's, and all that is
in it, the world, and all who live in it.*

PSALM 24:1

God created the world and filled it up with people. All kinds of people! He put them in different places, different countries all over the world. It's fun finding out about people who live near and far. You can explore the world right where you are by reading books about how people in other countries celebrate holidays, the kinds of food they enjoy, what clothing they wear. You can even talk with people in other countries by learning their languages. Everyone who believes in God is a member of His family. No matter where you live, you are His.

GOD, CREATOR OF EVERYTHING, THERE ARE SO MANY NEW FRIENDS IN THE WORLD WAITING TO MEET ME. WILL YOU HELP US TO FIND ONE ANOTHER? AMEN.

I Can Talk with God

*"Then you will call upon Me and come
and pray to Me, and I will listen to you."*
JEREMIAH 29:12

God calls us His children. Even though the world is filled with people—billions of people!—each one is special to Him. God always has time for us, time to be alone with each of us. When we pray, we are talking with God. Can you imagine all the children in the world praying in their own languages? God hears every prayer as if it is the only one. He is amazing! He is everywhere all the time; still, we can be alone with God whenever we want just by saying a prayer.

FATHER GOD, HERE I AM. I KNOW YOU ARE
LISTENING. YOU WANT TO HEAR MY PRAYERS.
LET'S HAVE SOME QUIET TIME TOGETHER, AND
I'LL TELL YOU ALL ABOUT MY DAY. AMEN.

God Loves Us

I love those who love me, and those who
look for me with much desire will find me.

PROVERBS 8:17

God's love is big. It is endless! He loves every one of
His children. God doesn't love us because of how we
look, what we have, where we live, or what we know.
He looks inside our hearts. He loves us because we
love Him. When we fill our hearts with love for God,
we want more of Him. We want to learn about Him and
please Him in everything we do. Ask God to fill up your
heart with love.

DEAR GOD, YOU LOVE ME JUST THE WAY I AM RIGHT
NOW. I DON'T HAVE TO BE OR DO ANYTHING SPECIAL
TO EARN YOUR LOVE. YOU LOVE ME BECAUSE I AM
YOURS. I LOVE YOU TOO, GOD. KEEP FILLING MY
HEART WITH YOUR ENDLESS LOVE. AMEN.

God Gave Us Jesus

"For God so loved the world that He gave His only Son. Whoever puts his trust in God's Son will not be lost but will have life that lasts forever."
JOHN 3:16

Because God loves us, He sent His Son, Jesus, into the world to save us from our sin. Sometimes we do things that don't please God. Instead of punishing us, God allowed Jesus to take the punishment we deserve. Jesus was okay with that because He loves us. When we give our lives to Jesus, He sends His Holy Spirit to come and live within us forever. Someday when we die, we will live with Jesus in heaven. Did you know Jesus is your very best friend? He will never leave you or let you down.

DEAR JESUS, THANK YOU FOR BEING MY BEST FRIEND AND FOR SENDING YOUR HOLY SPIRIT TO LIVE IN MY HEART FOREVER. AMEN.

Love Each Other

"This is what I tell you to do: Love each other."
JOHN 15:17

Jesus said many important things when He lived on earth. You can read about them in the Bible. He taught us to live in ways that please God. He said we should love one another the way God loves us, with kind and forgiving hearts. God wants us to live in peace with one another all the time. He is also pleased when we help one another to show love and do good deeds (see Hebrews 10:24). Can you think of a few ways you can help others to get along better and love one another?

DEAR GOD, PLEASE HELP ME TO LOVE OTHERS THE WAY YOU LOVE THEM. I PROMISE TO DO MY BEST TO BRING MORE PEACE AND LOVE INTO THE WORLD. AMEN.

The Bible Is for Everyone

Man is helped when he is taught God's Word.
It shows what is wrong. It changes the way of a
man's life. It shows him how to be right with God.
2 TIMOTHY 3:16

The Bible is sometimes called "God's Word." Everything in it comes from God. The Bible teaches us how God wants us to live. The Bible is about all kinds of people—people who are different in many different ways. Some of its stories show us how to get along and live at peace with one another. The Bible teaches us what God says is right and wrong. When we put into action what we learn from the Bible, our love for God and others grows stronger all the time.

HEAVENLY FATHER, WHEN I READ THE BIBLE, TEACH ME MORE ABOUT YOU AND HOW YOU WANT ME TO LIVE. AMEN.

What Do You See?

I will give thanks to You, for the greatness of the way I was made. . . . Your works are great and my soul knows it very well.

PSALM 139:14

When God creates people, He decides what they will look like. Stand in front of a mirror and look at yourself. What do you see? What color is your hair? Your skin? What color are your eyes? God made you and everyone else beautiful—precious in His sight. When you look at your family members, friends, and neighbors, you can imagine them as God's works of art. Each person looks a little bit different, even twins do! Blue eyes, brown eyes, red hair, black hair, light skin, dark skin—God made no two people exactly alike.

DEAR GOD, I LIKE ME JUST THE WAY I AM.
THANK YOU FOR MAKING ME BEAUTIFUL. AMEN.

God Looks at the Heart

"The Lord does not look at the things man looks at. A man looks at the outside of a person, but the Lord looks at the heart."

1 SAMUEL 16:7

When meeting someone, the first thing you might notice is what that person looks like. It's easy to focus on what you see. But God wants you to look at what you can't see! That sounds funny, doesn't it? How can you look at what you can't see? The Bible explains it like this: God doesn't care as much about what people look like as He cares about what's inside their hearts—how they behave. He wants us to "see" the good in people— kindness, forgiveness, love. Can you think of other good things you might see in others?

LORD, HELP ME TO SEE THE GOOD IN PEOPLE. AMEN.

Respect One Another

Love each other as Christian brothers.
Show respect for each other.
ROMANS 12:10

"Respect" means treating others in a kind and caring way. It can also mean not complaining when obeying your parents, teachers, and most of all, God. Saying mean things about someone is never respectful. Neither is making fun of someone or treating them badly because of how they behave, what they look like, where they come from—or any other reason. Everyone deserves respect. God is pleased when we show respect for one another. Think about this: If you saw someone being disrespected or you heard someone say something bad about someone, what would you do?

DEAR GOD, FORGIVE ME FOR THOSE TIMES
WHEN I'VE BEEN DISRESPECTFUL. HELP ME
TO SHOW RESPECT FOR OTHERS EVEN WHEN I
THINK THEY DON'T DESERVE IT. TEACH ME TO
BE A GOOD EXAMPLE OF SOMEONE WHO
IS CARING AND KIND. AMEN.

Celebrate!

God has given each of you a gift. Use it to help each other. This will show God's loving-favor.
1 PETER 4:10

God gives each of us skills and talents—things we are good at. Maybe you've clapped for a friend's performance in a concert or play, or cheered when a friend won a race. It's important to celebrate the different ways people are good at things and to say, "Great job!" But it's even more important to remember that God is the reason for our accomplishments. He is the One who makes us able, and He deserves our thanks. We should use what we're good at to honor Him and help others. What are you good at?

FATHER, THANK YOU FOR GIVING ME SKILLS AND TALENTS, THINGS I DO WELL. WHENEVER I ACCOMPLISH SOMETHING GOOD, I WILL CELEBRATE YOU, BECAUSE YOU MADE ME ABLE TO DO IT. AMEN.

May I Help You?

Let each of you look out not only for his own interests, but also for the interests of others.
PHILIPPIANS 2:4 NKJV

Have you needed help with something but felt afraid to ask? Maybe you didn't want people to know you needed help. All of us need one another's help sometimes. It's perfectly okay to ask. Keep your eyes open for others in need. They might be uncomfortable asking too. You could step right up and say, "May I help you?" And you might add, "I need help sometimes too." Remember that we're all sisters and brothers in God's big family. He wants us to look out for and help one another.

DEAR GOD, WHEN I NEED HELP, GIVE ME COURAGE TO ASK. I KNOW YOU ARE ALWAYS READY TO HELP ME, AND YOU'VE PUT OTHERS ALL AROUND ME WHO ARE WILLING TO HELP TOO. AMEN.

Listen to Us Sing

Sing praise to the Lord, all you who belong to Him. Give thanks to His holy name.

PSALM 30:4

A choir is a group of people singing together. Imagine all the kids in the world singing together in their many different languages. Think of them singing songs of praise to God because they love Him. God loves all the world's children. He loves hearing His children sing. He understands every single word in every language. You don't need a beautiful singing voice or to be in a choir to sing praise songs to God. Right where you are, right this very minute, you can make up a song and sing it to Him. Will you do it? Sing a song and tell God you love Him.

DEAR HEAVENLY FATHER, I WILL SING
A LOVE SONG TO YOU TODAY. AMEN.

Good Job!

"You have done well. You are a
good and faithful servant."
MATTHEW 25:21

We feel good when we hear people say nice things about us. When we say something nice about someone, it's called a "compliment." Compliments are one way we show love and respect for one another. Jesus told a story in which a man gave an important job to his workers. One worker did an especially good job. The man complimented him, saying, "You have done well. You are a good and faithful servant." That is what we should say to others: "You did a great job!" There are many nice things we can say about the things people accomplish. Can you think of a few?

DEAR GOD, PLEASE HELP ME TO NOTICE WHEN SOMEONE
DOES SOMETHING GOOD. EVERY DAY I WANT TO GIVE
LOTS AND LOTS OF COMPLIMENTS. AMEN.

You Have a Beautiful Heart

Your beauty should come from the inside.
It should come from the heart.

1 PETER 3:4

Most of the time, people compliment one another about the way they look: their choice of clothes, how they wear their hair, the glasses they wear, the color of their eyes or skin. Everyone has something beautiful on the outside to notice. But what's even more beautiful is what's inside a person's heart. That's where things like love, kindness, forgiveness, and courage live. You can see inside a person's heart by the ways he or she behaves. When you see someone do something loving, kind, or courageous, that's worth a compliment! What other good things do you think are inside a person's heart?

FATHER GOD, WHEN I SEE GOOD THINGS IN SOMEONE'S HEART, REMIND ME TO LET THEM KNOW. AMEN.

Jesus Loves Us!

Jesus said, "Let the little children come to Me. Do not stop them. The holy nation of heaven is made up of ones like these."
MATTHEW 19:14

Maybe you have been with a bunch of grown-ups and felt they weren't paying much attention to you. The Bible tells us that crowds often followed Jesus, wanting to hear what He said. Kids were there with their parents. They might have felt a little lost and alone among all those grown-ups. But Jesus saw them. He said, "Let the little children come to Me." Jesus loves kids—all kids, all around the world. Jesus loves *you*! Wherever you are, you can talk with Him in prayer. Just bow your head, fold your hands, and begin, "Dear Jesus. . ."

DEAR JESUS, THANK YOU FOR ALWAYS WELCOMING ME AND FOR LOVING ALL THE KIDS IN THE WORLD. AMEN.

Can You Count the Stars?

[God] took [Abram] outside and said, "Now look up into the heavens and add up the stars, if you are able to number them." Then He said to him, "Your children and your children's children will be as many as the stars."

GENESIS 15:5

Long ago God asked a man named Abram if he could count all the stars. Of course Abram couldn't—there are way too many! God promised Abram that he would have lots of children. And his children would have children. And their children would have children. And on and on. The world is always filled with God's children. Kids live in every country of the world, and in many ways they are just like you.

DEAR GOD, YOU HAVE CREATED ALL CHILDREN.
HELP ME TO SEE THE WAYS I AM LIKE EVERY
OTHER CHILD IN THE WORLD. AMEN.

Everything Is Beautiful

All flesh is not the same. Men have one kind of flesh. Animals have another kind. Fish have another kind, and birds have another kind.

1 CORINTHIANS 15:39

When God created animals, He gave their fur different colors and patterns. Pandas are black and white, flamingoes are pink, zebras have stripes, leopards have spots. Fish have scales in different colors—some fish are gray, others, like goldfish, are orange, white, and red. Some even have scales that shine like a rainbow in sunlight. God made birds with feathers in almost every color you can imagine. And when God made people, He gave them different skin colors. Everyone's skin is beautiful. Everything God made is beautiful.

HEAVENLY FATHER, YOU MADE US ALL TO LOOK
DIFFERENT, AND THAT IS WHAT MAKES THE WORLD
A BEAUTIFUL PLACE. WHATEVER SKIN WE ARE IN,
IT IS PERFECT AND RIGHT AND LOVELY. AMEN.

You Have a Colorful Personality

We are to grow up and be more like Christ.
EPHESIANS 4:15

God gives us different personalities—different ways of thinking, feeling, and behaving that blend together like the colors in a rainbow and make each of us one of a kind. You were born with all the good things in your heart that God wants you to be. But life can get in the way of those good things and cause you to behave badly. God wants you always to try to be like Jesus. Jesus cares about and helps people. He tells the truth. He finishes what He starts. Jesus is patient, loving, and kind. When not-so-good things creep into your personality, stop yourself from doing what you know is wrong. Try to be more like Jesus.

DEAR JESUS, HELP ME TO BE MORE LIKE YOU. AMEN.

Let's All Get Along

As much as you can, live in peace with all men.
ROMANS 12:18

Differences in our personalities can make us want to fight, argue, and disagree with one another.

Imagine this: While sitting in school you look at your feet and see one purple sock and one blue sock. Those different socks don't match. Sometimes our colorful personalities clash like a mismatched pair of socks. People don't always get along. But Jesus wants us to do our best to get along with and to live in peace with one another. Is there someone whose personality is different from yours, someone you find hard to get along with? What could you do to make things better?

DEAR JESUS, I DON'T GET ALONG WITH SOME PEOPLE. HELP ME TO THINK ABOUT HOW WE ARE ALIKE INSTEAD OF HOW WE ARE DIFFERENT. HELP US TO LIVE IN PEACE. AMEN.

"Hello!"

A friend loves at all times.

PROVERBS 17:17

Who are your friends? Can you list their names? Where did you meet them? How are you alike and how are you different? Friendship is something that starts with one simple word: *Hello*. As you get to know new friends, you'll discover all kinds of wonderful things about them. You learn what you have in common. And you'll discover differences too. Those differences will help you to learn new things about the world and one another. Always be on the lookout for new friends. You'll find them everywhere—at school, at church, in your neighborhood. Just step right up and say, "Hello!"

DEAR GOD, THANK YOU FOR MY FRIENDS. I LOVE THEM! WE HAVE SO MUCH FUN TOGETHER. I'D LIKE TO MAKE SOME NEW FRIENDS TOO. LEAD ME TO THEM, GOD. I WANT TO SAY, "HELLO!" AMEN.

We Work Together

*Two are better than one. . . . If one of
them falls, the other can help him up.*
ECCLESIASTES 4:9–10

Think about this: Could you play soccer all by yourself?
Could you play a board game alone or talk with someone
on a video call? Some things need two or more people.
That's why it's great to have friends. When friends work
together, they not only have fun, but they get things
done. Friends help one another. Friends working together discover ideas for helping in their communities.
They see ways they can make life better for old people,
the homeless, and others. Can you think of a way you
and your friends might work together to help someone?

FATHER GOD, I HAVE A WHOLE TEAM OF FRIENDS!
WHAT CAN WE DO TO HELP OTHERS? WE'RE
READY, GOD. SHOW US THE WAY. AMEN.

Share the Good News

*[Jesus] said to them, "You are to go to all the world
and preach the Good News to every person."*

MARK 16:15

Jesus said we should tell the Good News to everyone in
the world. What's the Good News? It's this: Jesus is a
forever friend to all who believe in Him. The Bible books
Matthew, Mark, Luke, and John tell Jesus' story. Learning about Him helps us to see how God wants us to live
and also how we can live with God in heaven someday.
From when Jesus lived on earth until now, people have
shared the Good News. Jesus loves you. He loves all kids.
You can help your friends know Jesus by sharing with
them that He wants to be their friend forever.

DEAR JESUS, I WANT EVERYONE IN THE WORLD TO KNOW
YOU. PLEASE HELP ME TO SHARE THE GOOD NEWS. AMEN.

We're One Big Family

God does not see you as a Jew or as a Greek.
He does not see you as a servant or as a
person free to work. He does not see you as a
man or as a woman. You are all one in Christ.
GALATIANS 3:28

Some families are made up of children adopted from different parts of the world. Some families have people with different skin colors. Family members come in all sizes—tall, short, and everything in between. Some have disabilities that make life a little more challenging. Families live in all kinds of houses in many different neighborhoods. Even with all the differences, God sees everyone the same. We are all equal in His sight.

DEAR GOD, YOU LOVE ALL OF US THE SAME.
THAT'S HOW I WANT TO LOVE OTHERS TOO. AMEN.

God Knows My Name

He knows the number of the stars.
He gives names to all of them.

PSALM 147:4

Could you count all the stars in the sky? Of course not—there are too many! But God knows exactly how many there are. God gave each star a name. He knows your name too. He knows the names of every man, woman, and child on earth: Mateo, Tamar, Haruto, Magret, Noah, Emma. . . God knows everyone's name. Give this a try. Say the names of everyone you know. As you say them, count the names. It took awhile, didn't it? God knows everyone's name right now without even counting. Isn't He amazing?

HEAVENLY FATHER, I WISH I KNEW WHAT NAMES
YOU GAVE TO THE STARS. BUT SOME THINGS I
CAN'T KNOW UNTIL I MEET YOU IN HEAVEN ONE
DAY. I'M GLAD YOU KNOW MY NAME. AMEN.

Where Do You Come From?

Praise the Lord, all nations! Praise Him, all people!
PSALM 117:1

Because you are born in a certain country doesn't mean you will stay there. People like to travel. Sometimes they travel for many miles to live in another country far away. Maybe you know someone who came from another place. That person might have interesting stories to tell. You could ask questions like these: Where did you come from? What was your favorite thing about living there? What is different about living here? People come from all over the world—different cities, states, and countries—yet they are all part of God's good creation.

DEAR GOD, WHEN I MEET A NEW FRIEND FROM ANOTHER CITY, STATE, OR COUNTRY, REMIND ME TO ASK QUESTIONS ABOUT WHERE THEY CAME FROM. FINDING OUT ABOUT EACH OTHER CAN HELP TO MAKE US BETTER FRIENDS. AMEN.

I Will Pray for You

I always give thanks for you and pray for you.
EPHESIANS 1:16

When you pray, what do you and God talk about? One of the best gifts you can give a person is to pray for him or her. Friends, family members, kids at school, your teachers, community helpers, even people you don't know—all of them are helped by your prayers. You can ask God to help with whatever they need. You can ask Him to help those who are sick, sad, or lonely. You can ask Him to help someone accomplish something. You can ask God to keep a person safe. You can pray for people all over the world, people you've never met— those who are poor and hungry and those who don't know Jesus. Think about it—who can you pray for today?

FATHER GOD, LEAD ME TO PRAY FOR OTHERS TODAY. AMEN.

Sometimes It's Hard to Pray

"But I tell you, love those who hate you. (Respect and give thanks for those who say bad things to you. Do good to those who hate you.) Pray for those who do bad things to you and who make it hard for you."

MATTHEW 5:44

People don't always get along. When someone disrespects you, says bad things about you, or makes it hard for you, what should you do? Jesus says to love that person by trying your best to be good to him or her. And also—to pray. If someone treats you badly, tell Jesus. He understands how you feel. Ask Him to help you to pray for others. Praying can help you to feel better. When you treat people with caring and respect, then God will be pleased with you.

DEAR GOD, HELP ME TO PRAY FOR THOSE
WHO DISRESPECT AND HURT ME. AMEN.

I Listen with My Heart

He whose ear listens to careful words
spoken will live among the wise.

PROVERBS 15:31

Have you argued with your brother or sister because you disagreed about something? Did you end up yelling at each other until your parent said, "Stop"? Today's Bible verse reminds us to listen to one another. When you listen, you should listen with your heart. That means doing your best to understand not only the words you hear but also the feelings behind them. When you put together careful words and a listening heart, fewer arguments will happen. The next time you feel like arguing, practice listening with your heart. Choose your words carefully. Then see what happens.

HEAVENLY FATHER, I'M NOT ALWAYS THE BEST LISTENER. I ARGUE SOMETIMES WITHOUT LISTENING. HELP ME LEARN TO HEAR WITH MY HEART AND TO BE CAREFUL WHEN CHOOSING MY WORDS. AMEN.

We Love Holidays!

This is the day that the Lord has made.
Let us be full of joy and be glad in it.
PSALM 118:24

Holidays are special days when we celebrate something. There are many different holidays. Christians celebrate Christmas, the day Jesus was born, and Easter, the day He came alive after being crucified on the cross. Jewish friends celebrate Hanukkah, remembering a time when God made one day's worth of lamp oil last eight days. Kwanzaa is a special time when people celebrate African American traditions. Almost everyone in the world celebrates a new year, but in different ways: in Spain, eating twelve grapes at midnight; in Demark, standing on chairs and jumping off at midnight into the new year. Families have different ways of celebrating holidays. Ask your friends how they celebrate. You might learn something new!

THANK YOU, GOD, FOR HOLIDAYS,
FAMILIES, FRIENDS, AND FUN. AMEN.

It's a Brand-New Day

I will honor You every day, and praise
Your name forever and ever.

PSALM 145:2

God plans each day with new things for you to discover. Keep your eyes open, because He hides His little surprises. Maybe today you'll find a pretty butterfly on the petals of a flower or see a cloud in the shape of a hippopotamus. Today you might make friends with someone new or learn something new about an old friend. You and your friend could learn something new together. Every day is a fresh beginning. If yesterday wasn't so good, if you disobeyed your parent or argued with your sister, God gives you another chance today to make things better. God gave you today because He loves you. At the end of each day, tell Him thank You.

DEAR GOD, THANK YOU FOR TODAY AND
NEW THINGS TO DISCOVER. AMEN.

What Is a Disability?

Jesus answered, ". . .He was born blind so the work of God would be seen in him."

JOHN 9:3

When Jesus was asked why the man was born blind, He answered, "So the work of God would be seen in him." There are some things that people with disabilities need to work a little harder at. But God helps them! The blind can't see; still, God helps them to do a thousand other things and do them well. Everyone has something they have to work harder at. Can you think of something that isn't easy for you? Ask God to help you. And if you meet someone who has a disability, God wants you to see what they *can* do, not what they can't.

HEAVENLY FATHER, PEOPLE WITH DISABILITIES
ARE JUST LIKE ME—WE ALL NEED YOUR HELP
SOMETIMES TO GET THINGS DONE. AMEN.

What Do You Need?

Help each other in troubles and problems.
This is the kind of law Christ asks us to obey.
GALATIANS 6:2

Jesus always knows exactly what kind of help we need. He doesn't have to think about it; He just knows. People are different. Some needs are easy for us to spot and help with. (For example, if Mom has four grocery bags to carry and she can only hold two, you can help carry the rest.) Other needs are harder to spot. If a friend seems angry, upset, or sad, you might have to ask, "Are you okay? Is there something you need?" Each time you show you care, you become a little more like Jesus.

FATHER GOD, HELP ME TO NOTICE WHEN THE PEOPLE
AROUND ME NEED HELP. AND IF I'M NOT SURE,
REMIND ME THAT IT'S OKAY TO ASK. AMEN.

Jesus Is Always with Me

"I am with you always, even to the end of the world."
MATTHEW 28:20

The Bible books Matthew, Mark, Luke, and John tell about Jesus' life on earth. Before Jesus left earth and went back to heaven to be with His Father, God, Jesus told His friends, "I am with you always." You can't see Him, but Jesus is with you all the time. He is with God. He is a part of God. Jesus sees you, and He knows you. Jesus is gentle, good, and kind. He is everything God wants you to be. As you learn about Jesus, work at becoming more like Him. You can pray and talk with Jesus anytime. He is your helper and friend—and He loves you.

DEAR JESUS, I WANT TO LEARN MORE ABOUT
YOU SO I CAN BECOME MORE LIKE YOU. AMEN.

Jesus Is the Super-est Superhero!

Jesus came and said to them, "All power has been given to Me in heaven and on earth."
MATTHEW 28:18

Superheroes exist in books, the movies, and on TV. These make-believe characters have superhuman powers. Some superheroes are super strong or super fast. Others can fly, change shape, or become invisible. It's fun to watch them, but you should remember that they're not real. Jesus is real, and He has real superpowers. God has given Jesus all power in heaven and on earth. By the Holy Spirit, Jesus can be everywhere all the time. He sees you and hears your prayers. He is able to do anything! Whenever you need help, you can always trust Jesus. He isn't just the super-est of all superheroes—Jesus is your very best friend.

JESUS, I KNOW YOU ARE REAL. YOU CAN DO ANYTHING. YOU ARE MY BEST FRIEND, AND I TRUST YOU. AMEN.

Let's Share

All those who put their trust in Christ were together and shared what they owned.

ACTS 2:44

When you were little and someone wanted to play with your favorite toy, you held on to it and said, "No!" But you are older now, and you understand that it's good to share. Imagine that you and Dad are in the kitchen making a pizza. You begin putting on the toppings. Then your little brother says, "My turn!" You want to make the pizza your way, but you remember to share and let your brother help. God is pleased when you share with others. There are many different ways of sharing. You can share your things, your chores, your time, what you learn. What will you share today?

DEAR GOD, WHEN I DON'T FEEL LIKE SHARING, HELP ME TO REMEMBER THAT SHARING PLEASES GOD. AMEN.

"Hola!"

There are many languages in the world. All of them have meaning to the people who understand them.
1 CORINTHIANS 14:10

Antonio is a new boy in class.

"Say hello to Antonio," says the teacher.

The class answers, "Hello, Antonio!"

Antonio says, "Hola!"

Antonio is from Mexico, and in his country "Hola" means "Hello." Maybe you know someone who grew up in another country. The words they use and the way they speak might sound strange to you. But think about this: The way you speak sounds strange to them! Kids around the world speak many languages. The words they use, how they speak, is one way kids are different. Now can you think of some ways all children are alike?

DEAR JESUS, WHATEVER LANGUAGE WE SPEAK, YOU UNDERSTAND US. IN YOUR SIGHT WE ARE ALL EQUAL. WE ARE YOUR CREATION, AND YOU LOVE US. AMEN.

I Like It! I Don't Like It!

*A dish of vegetables with love is better
than eating the best meat with hate.*

PROVERBS 15:17

What kind of food don't you want anywhere near your lips? Which is your favorite food? Everyone has things they like and dislike. Your friend likes puppies; you prefer kittens. Your aunt dyes purple streaks in her hair; your mom likes her hair blond, just as it is. There are many things people like and dislike, and that's okay unless their differences cause them to dislike one another. Jesus said we should love one another. Sometimes that means putting our differences aside and trying to get along by thinking more about how we are alike than how we are different.

THANK YOU, GOD, FOR TEACHING ME THAT IT'S OKAY TO HAVE DIFFERENT OPINIONS AS LONG AS WE ALL GET ALONG. AMEN.

I Give to the World

Each has his own gift from God. One has one gift. Another has another gift.
1 CORINTHIANS 7:7

Paul was a follower of Jesus who wrote part of the Bible. Paul was good at teaching and writing. He also gave excellent advice. Paul said that God gives each of us gifts—things we do well. He said some people are good at helping and others are good at making people feel better. Some are good at sharing, being kind, or teaching others. God gives all of us different things we do well so that we can use those gifts to make the world a better place. Think about your God-given gifts. How could you use them to help others?

DEAR GOD, SHOW ME HOW TO USE MY GIFTS.
I WANT TO SHARE THEM WITH THE WORLD. AMEN.

What Does "Precious" Mean?

"Since you were precious in My sight, You have been honored, and I have loved you."
ISAIAH 43:4 NKJV

The title of this book is *Precious in His Sight*. Have you wondered what the word *precious* means? Maybe you've heard someone say about a newborn baby, "Oh, isn't he precious!" Or maybe someone has said that about you. *Precious* is a loving word like *dear* or *sweetheart*. It also means "of great value." God loves you. You are dear to Him and of great value. You are His child. He wouldn't leave you or trade you for anything. Jesus sees you as special, one of a kind, created by God. You and all the children in the world are precious in His sight.

DEAR JESUS, YOU MAKE ME FEEL SO SPECIAL. I CAN FEEL YOUR LOVE IN MY HEART, AND I LOVE YOU TOO. AMEN.

I Feel Jesus' Love

*Our life is lived by faith. We do not
live by what we see in front of us.*
2 CORINTHIANS 5:7

You can't see love, but you can feel it. When you receive a big, warm hug, you know love is real. Jesus is like a hug. You can't see Him, but you can feel Him loving you. The Bible says Jesus is real. He lived on earth. When Jesus went back to heaven, He promised to be with us always. You can't see Him, but you can feel His love all around you. Jesus' love lives inside your heart. *Faith* is a word that means we believe in something we can't see. Do you have faith that Jesus loves you?

DEAR JESUS, WHEN I TALK WITH YOU THROUGH
PRAYER, I FEEL YOUR LOVE IN MY HEART. I HAVE
FAITH THAT YOU ARE ALWAYS WITH ME. AMEN.

I Know How You Feel

Be happy with those who are happy.
Be sad with those who are sad.
ROMANS 12:15

You can't see feelings, but they are always there swirling around inside you. There are many different feelings: happy, sad, brave, sick, afraid, angry, bored. Can you think of several more? Although you can't see feelings, you can often tell how someone feels by how he or she behaves. Jesus was great at understanding people's feelings. You can become more like Him by noticing when someone seems sad, afraid, angry, or sick and then doing your best to help. Remember to look for the good feelings too. Feelings like happy, silly, thankful, and proud are wonderful feelings to share.

DEAR GOD, PLEASE HELP ME TO BECOME
BETTER AT NOTICING HOW OTHER PEOPLE ARE
FEELING. I WANT TO SHOW THEM I CARE. AMEN.

I'm So Angry!

A man with a bad temper starts fights,
but he who is slow to anger quiets fighting.

PROVERBS 15:18

Do you ever get angry with your brothers, sisters, parents, or friends? Most kids do. Everyone gets angry sometimes. Feeling angry in itself isn't a bad thing, but what you do with an angry feeling can get you into trouble. If you let anger cause you to yell at someone or say bad things about them, that's not good! Today's Bible verse says that slowing down an angry feeling quiets fighting. The next time you feel angry, try to slow down the feeling and avoid a fight. Learning to calm your anger is one of the best things you can do to become better at getting along with others.

HEAVENLY FATHER, WHENEVER I GET AN ANGRY FEELING, PLEASE TEACH ME TO GO SLOW AND QUIET IT DOWN. AMEN.

I Forgive You

*"Forgive other people and other
people will forgive you."*
LUKE 6:37

We feel sad when people show anger toward us or hurt our feelings. We want them not only to say they are sorry but also to show us they mean it. When someone is truly sorry, it's easier for us to forgive. But what if a person isn't sorry? Jesus said, "Forgive other people and other people will forgive you." He had even more to say about forgiveness. When Jesus was asked how many times we should forgive someone, He said, "Seventy times seven" (Matthew 18:22). He meant we should keep on forgiving. How are you at forgiveness? Could you keep forgiving someone who hurt you?

DEAR GOD, HELP ME TO FORGIVE OTHERS. FORGIVING DOESN'T
MEAN I HAVE TO BELIEVE WHAT THEY DID WAS RIGHT, BUT
FORGIVENESS MAKES ME RIGHT WITH YOU. AMEN.

I Want to Be Right with God

*Remember to do good and help each
other. Gifts like this please God.*
HEBREWS 13:16

When you are right with God, you become better at getting along with others. Being right with God means doing your best to please Him. Whenever you feel like misbehaving, you should ask yourself, *Will that please God?* If the answer is no, then you can work at turning your behavior around. You will please God when you are helpful, treat others with respect, and do what is good. Remember—God sees everything, and when you behave well and treat others well, it's like giving Him a gift. What can you do to please God today?

I WANT TO BE RIGHT WITH YOU, GOD. I WILL DO
MY VERY BEST TO DO WHAT IS GOOD, CHECK MY
BEHAVIOR, AND TREAT OTHERS WELL. AMEN.

I Will Be a Peacemaker

"Those who make peace are happy,
because they will be called the sons of God."
MATTHEW 5:9

"Those who make peace are happy." That's what Jesus said! When people get along, it's a good day. There's no arguing or fighting. Everything feels peaceful. When we get along with others, we feel good inside. Did you know that you can be a peacemaker? You can bring peace to others by doing your best to get along and by being helpful. If you have a friend who's grumpy or sad, show that you care. If your mom is tired after a long day at work, bring her some peace by helping out and behaving well. Practice being a peacemaker. See if it makes you happy today.

DEAR GOD, I WANT TO BE A PEACEMAKER. SHOW ME
WHAT I CAN DO TO HELP US ALL GET ALONG. AMEN.

That's Scary!

For God did not give us a spirit of fear. He gave us a spirit of power and of love and of a good mind.
2 TIMOTHY 1:7

Have you noticed that different people have different feelings? What one person finds scary might bring another person joy. Maybe you run when you see a big, hairy spider. Your friend might think the spider is neat and take a closer look. Maybe that same friend is afraid of deep water, but you aren't afraid—you love to swim. The Bible says more than two hundred times, "Fear not." When you put your trust in Jesus, you don't have to be afraid. You can trust Him to help you to feel peaceful inside. Tell your friends about Jesus so they can trust in Him too.

DEAR JESUS, WHENEVER I AM AFRAID,
I CAN TRUST YOU TO HELP ME. AMEN.

We Depend on One Another

There are many people who belong to Christ.
And yet, we are one body which is Christ's.
We are all different but we depend on each other.
ROMANS 12:5

If you have a pet, it depends on you. Your pet expects you to feed it, give it water, and even provide a bathroom. It depends on you for playtime, cuddles, and love. Everyone depends on someone for something. You depend on your parents to love you and provide a safe home. You depend on your teachers to help you learn. We are different in so many ways, yet we all need one another. There is One everybody can depend on—God! He loves us, differences and all, and He is always ready to meet our needs.

DEAR HEAVENLY FATHER, WHATEVER I NEED,
WHEREVER I AM, I KNOW I CAN DEPEND ON YOU. AMEN.

Will You Be My Friend?

*Be happy to have people stay for
the night and eat with you.*

1 PETER 4:9

When everything stays the same, we feel safe and comfortable. But when things become different, we might feel unsettled. Maybe your family moved someplace new and you had to say goodbye to your friends. Your new home felt uncomfortable because it was different. Different can be good! Different often means an exciting new adventure. It can mean turning strangers into friends. Always be ready to welcome new people into your life. When you invite new friends to join you, they can teach you all kinds of different and fun things that you can enjoy together.

DEAR GOD, WHEN DIFFERENT FEELS A LITTLE BIT SCARY, WILL
YOU REMIND ME THAT DIFFERENT CAN BE GOOD? I WANT
TO MAKE NEW FRIENDS AND LEARN NEW THINGS. AMEN.

God Knows All about Me

"God knows how many hairs you have on your head."
MATTHEW 10:30

How many hairs are on your head? That seems like a silly question. Whoever would take time to count them all? The Bible says God knows how many hairs are up there. And if a few hairs end up on your comb, God knows that too. He knows everything about you, even the tiniest things that you don't notice. He knows every beat of your heart and every thought in your brain. He knows about and understands all your feelings. And God doesn't just know everything about *you*—He knows everything about everyone on earth. That's just one of the reasons He is so great.

GOD, YOU MUST REALLY LOVE ME TO WANT TO KNOW EVERY LITTLE THING ABOUT ME. I FEEL SAFE KNOWING HOW MUCH YOU CARE. AMEN.

Our Bodies Are Different

*I praise you because of the wonderful
way you created me.*
PSALM 139:14 CEV

God made each of our bodies in a wonderful way. Each body is different. When you look at your friends, you will see all kinds of little differences. Some people use their left hand more than their right. If you and your friends lined up your fingerprints on a piece of paper, you would see that no two fingerprints are alike. Some people have naturally curly hair, others have straight hair. Eye colors are different and even the shapes of eyes can be different. God put all our body parts together just the way He wanted so no two of us would be exactly alike.

DEAR GOD, YOU CREATED OUR BODIES TO LOOK DIFFERENT
AND BEAUTIFUL. YOU PUT OUR BODY PARTS TOGETHER
IN A GREAT AND WONDERFUL WAY. AMEN.

What Are You Wearing?

"Do not say what is wrong in other people's lives. Then other people will not say what is wrong in your life."
MATTHEW 7:1

How people decide to dress depends on where they live and who they are. If you live in a place that's hot, you would be comfortable in shorts and a T-shirt. If you live where it's cold, boots, mittens, and a heavy coat would keep you warm. Wherever you live, you choose your own style to show your personality: bright colors, a favorite color, patterns, jeans. . . You not only dress to look good, but you dress to feel comfortable. Never make fun of someone's style. It's one of those differences that makes each of us special.

FATHER GOD, I'M GRATEFUL WE ALL HAVE OUR OWN SPECIAL STYLE. IT MAKES THE WORLD A MORE BEAUTIFUL PLACE. AMEN.

I Show Others How to Behave

Let no one show little respect for you because you are young. Show other Christians how to live by your life. They should be able to follow you in the way you talk and in what you do.

1 TIMOTHY 4:12

Wherever you go, people see how you behave. If you behave well, you set an example for other kids by showing them ways to behave that please God. Jesus' follower Paul wrote a letter to his young friend Timothy. Paul told Timothy that the words he used and the ways he behaved would teach other Christians how to live. One of the most important things you can do is show others how to behave. Give it a try today.

DEAR GOD, I WILL TRY MY BEST TO BEHAVE IN WAYS THAT PLEASE YOU AND SET A GOOD EXAMPLE FOR OTHERS. AMEN.

Take the Right Path

*Do not go on the path of the sinful. Do not walk
in the way of bad men. Stay away from it.
Do not pass by it. Turn from it, and pass on.*
PROVERBS 4:14-15

Has someone wanted you to go along with him or her and do something you know is wrong? You aren't alone. Everyone wants to do wrong things sometimes. When that happens, it's important to follow that little voice in your heart that says, "No!" If a friend asks you to do something bad, don't be afraid to walk away. That's what the Bible says to do—stay away from it, turn from it. But if you do mess up, ask God to forgive you. He will. All the time.

HEAVENLY FATHER, HELP ME TO TAKE THE RIGHT PATH BY SAYING NO TO ANY BEHAVIOR I KNOW IS WRONG. AMEN.

What If I Mess Up?

If we tell Him our sins, He is faithful and we can depend on Him to forgive us of our sins.
1 JOHN 1:9

You had a bad day. You went down the wrong path and did something that displeased God. So, now what? The good news is that you can make it all better! When you do something you know is wrong, if you are sorry and talk with God about it, He will forgive you. Today's Bible verse says we can depend on God to forgive our sins—the bad things we do. Jesus told us to forgive others again and again, and that is exactly what God does. He won't just forgive you one time. God will never stop forgiving you when you mess up.

DEAR GOD, I MESSED UP TODAY, AND I'M
SORRY. PLEASE FORGIVE ME. AMEN.

I Will Be Gentle

A gentle answer turns away anger,
but a sharp word causes anger.
PROVERBS 15:1

Are you gentle? Gentleness means acting in a way that is quiet, caring, and kind. If someone is sad or sick, you act gently by not being loud and by showing you care. Did you know you can also be gentle with your words? "I understand." "How can I help?" Those are gentle words, the kind of words Jesus might use. Gentle words can help calm down anger. If your brother says angry words to you, should you say something mean back, or would it be better to say something like "Let's not fight"? The next time you feel like arguing or you aren't getting along, use some gentle words and see what happens.

DEAR JESUS, I WANT TO BE MORE LIKE YOU AND USE QUIET, GENTLE WORDS. WILL YOU HELP ME? AMEN.

Let's Be Helpers

Stand up for the rights of those
who are suffering and in need.
PSALM 82:3

All over the world there are kids and grown-ups who need things. Some need simple things like food, water, clothes, and a safe home to live in. Others live in countries where there are few schools and they need teachers, books, and supplies. Doctors are needed to help those who are sick. Along with needs you can see, everyone needs love and everyone needs Jesus. You and your friends can be God's helpers. Start by praying for those in need. Also, ask your parents, pastors, and teachers about ways to help. Maybe people you know, friends or neighbors, need help today. What could you do to meet their needs?

DEAR GOD, PLEASE GIVE OTHERS THE THINGS THEY
NEED, AND SHOW ME HOW TO HELP. AMEN.

May I Borrow That?

"If a person asks you for something, give it to him. Don't refuse to give to someone who wants to borrow from you."
MATTHEW 5:42 NCV

You got a neat *T. rex* model for your birthday. Your brother wants to borrow it for show and tell. What should you do? The Bible says to give to the one who asks you, and do not turn away from the one who wants to borrow from you. That means you shouldn't be selfish with your things. If you trust your brother to take care of your *T. rex*, then be a good giver and allow him to borrow it. God loves a cheerful giver! It's also important to be a good borrower and remember that the things you borrow don't belong to you.

DEAR JESUS, REMIND ME NOT ONLY TO BE AN UNSELFISH GIVER BUT ALSO A CAREFUL BORROWER. AMEN.

The Holy Spirit Guides Me

If you are guided by the Spirit,
you won't obey your selfish desires.
GALATIANS 5:16 CEV

God gives us the Holy Spirit to be our Helper. The Holy Spirit is part of who God is. The Holy Spirit is kind, patient, and gentle. His voice inside us reminds us of what's right and wrong. When we want to do something and we have a strong feeling that it's wrong, that's the Holy Spirit helping us. When we listen to that voice in our hearts and do what's right, we become more like Jesus. We learn to treat others the way Jesus does. Instead of thinking only about ourselves and what we want, we learn to be helpers and givers.

DEAR GOD, THANK YOU FOR SENDING THE HOLY
SPIRIT TO HELP ME. TEACH ME TO LISTEN
FOR YOUR SPIRIT IN MY HEART. AMEN.

What Is the Fruit of the Spirit?

But the fruit that comes from having the Holy Spirit in our lives is: love, joy, peace, not giving up, being kind, being good, having faith, being gentle, and being the boss over our own desires.

GALATIANS 5:22–23

Have you ever been apple picking? When an apple tree grows, it makes good fruit. The Holy Spirit gives us His own kind of "fruit"—it's some of the good things we see in Jesus, like love, peace, not giving up, being kind, being good, having faith, being gentle, and not giving in to what we know is wrong. The Holy Spirit helps us to become more like Jesus. The fruit of the Spirit helps us to love one another and get along.

DEAR GOD, PLEASE GIVE ME SOME OF THAT GOOD FRUIT SO I WILL BE MORE LIKE JESUS. AMEN.

I Am Joyful

"[God] will yet make you laugh and call out with joy."
JOB 8:21

Happiness is like unwrapping a present and finding something wonderful inside. Happiness comes from happy experiences like playing with your friends, winning a game, or getting a new pet. Some people use the word *joy* to mean "happy." But joy is different. Joy is an all-the-time feeling of peace in your heart even in unhappy times. The Bible says when we are unhappy we can still have joy in our hearts, knowing that Jesus loves us and is with us always. Whenever you feel sad, think about things that make you happy. Then thank God that sadness lasts just a little while. Soon you'll be happy again.

DEAR JESUS, WHEN I FEEL SAD, I'M JOYFUL KNOWING YOU ARE WITH ME AND YOU WILL HELP ME TO FEEL BETTER. AMEN.

Don't Give Up!

*I pray that God's great power will make
you strong, and that you will have joy
as you wait and do not give up.*

COLOSSIANS 1:11

You tried to do it and couldn't. You tried and tried, and then you said, "Maybe I'm just not old enough, strong enough, or big enough." Jesus' follower Paul said, "God's power makes us strong" (Colossians 1:11). You might have to wait a little while to do some of the things you want to do, but you can have joy while you wait because you're trusting God. He's working right now to make you old enough, strong enough, or big enough to do great things. Be patient. God loves you and will help you, so don't give up!

DEAR GOD, I TRIED TO DO IT, BUT I COULDN'T. PLEASE HELP ME
TO BE PATIENT UNTIL YOU SHOW ME THAT I CAN. AMEN.

I Will Teach You

*If someone has the gift of helping others,
then he should help. If someone has the
gift of teaching, he should teach.*

ROMANS 12:7

There are some things you can't do yet because you aren't old enough or strong enough. But there are many things you *can* do, and you can teach those things to others. If you can ride a bike, you can teach your younger sister or brother how to ride. If you know how to take care of a pet, you can teach a friend how to care for hers. You can teach what you know about Jesus and how to behave in ways that please God. Teach someone something today. Maybe there's something that person can teach you.

DEAR JESUS, WHO NEEDS ME TODAY? THERE ARE MANY THINGS I KNOW HOW TO DO, AND I WANT TO HELP. AMEN.

I'm the Boss over Me

*If the Holy Spirit is the boss over your
mind, it leads to life and peace.*
ROMANS 8:6

Who is the boss over you? Your mom? Your dad? Parents, teachers, and other grown-ups set the rules for kids. But you are the boss over you! You decide how to behave. The Holy Spirit is the voice in your heart that says, *"This is okay,"* or *"No. Stop!"* When the Holy Spirit speaks to you and you obey, you get a feeling of peace. You know what you did was right and pleasing to God. Get in the habit of listening for His voice in your heart. See if obeying Him helps you to behave even better.

DEAR GOD, TEACH ME TO LISTEN FOR AND TO
OBEY YOUR VOICE IN MY HEART. I WANT TO
DO WHAT IS RIGHT AND GOOD. AMEN.

Do What Is Right and Good

The Lord says, "Hold on to what is right and fair. Do what is right and good."

ISAIAH 56:1

Name three wrong things that people do. Now name three right things. People have different ideas about what is right or wrong. That's why it's important to know what God says. When you read the Bible, you learn what God expects from you. The Bible teaches us to hold on to good things like respect, kindness, forgiveness, and truthfulness. It teaches us to stay away from things like lies, acting rude, and being disrespectful and selfish. The Bible gives us Jesus as an example. Everything He did was right and good. Think about it: What right things did you do today?

HEAVENLY FATHER, TEACH ME THE DIFFERENCE
BETWEEN RIGHT AND WRONG SO I CAN BEHAVE
IN WAYS THAT PLEASE YOU. AMEN.

I'm Not Perfect

*This has become my way of life: When I want to
do what is right, I always do what is wrong.*
ROMANS 7:21

You had a fight with your best friend, you disrespected
your mom, and you forgot to finish your homework. You
wanted to please God by doing what was right, but you
ended up doing what was wrong. Does God still love
you? Of course He does! Nobody is perfect—except
God—and He doesn't expect you to be perfect. He is
pleased when you try your best to do what is right; and
when you do what is wrong, He forgives you. Be kind
to yourself when you mess up. Tomorrow is a new day,
and you will do better.

I'M GLAD YOU DON'T EXPECT ME TO BE PERFECT, GOD.
THANK YOU FOR LOVING ME JUST AS I AM. AMEN.

God Comes First

Do not love the world or anything in the world. If anyone loves the world, the Father's love is not in him.

1 JOHN 2:15

When something or someone is extra-special to you, it's hard to imagine anyone or anything being more important. But there is someone who should be. That someone is God. He made you, He loves you, and He watches over you all the time. God wants to be first in your life. When you put Him first, you show Him that you trust Him with everything and everyone you treasure. The things you love come and go, and they change. But God never leaves you, and He never changes. In fact, God makes everything you love even better.

DEAR GOD, I FORGET SOMETIMES THAT YOU ARE THE MOST IMPORTANT ONE IN MY LIFE. PLEASE FORGIVE ME. I LOVE YOU MORE THAN ANYTHING. AMEN.

Keep Going; You'll Get There

I run straight for the place at the end of the race. I fight to win. I do not beat the air.

1 CORINTHIANS 9:26

Watch how people run. Some go slow, others fast. Some take long steps, others little steps. People run at different speeds, but no matter how fast or slow, they end up reaching their goal. If you worry about reaching a goal—being able to do something like learning to ride a skateboard or play the piano or get better at reading—remember how fast you go isn't as important as getting there. Move at a speed that works for you. If you don't give up and if you fight to win, you will get to where you are going.

GOD, IF I WORRY ABOUT REACHING A GOAL, REMIND ME THAT SMALL, CAREFUL STEPS WILL GET ME THERE. AMEN.

I'm a Good Sport

*Anyone who runs in a race must
follow the rules to get the crown.*

2 TIMOTHY 2:5

How would you feel if your friend cheated when you
played a game? Cheating is wrong. If you cheat to win,
it takes all the fun out of a game. It's important to follow
the rules. When you do, it shows you are honest, and
that pleases God as well as those you are playing with.
You might not win by following the rules, but if you are
a good loser, others will respect you. A good loser is a
good sport—someone who is happy for whoever wins
the game. Think about it: Are you a good sport?

DEAR GOD, I DON'T LIKE TO LOSE, BUT WHEN I DO I TRY TO
BE A GOOD SPORT. WHEN I ACT HAPPY AND CONGRATULATE
THE WINNER, I KNOW IT PLEASES YOU. AMEN.

What Does "Humble" Mean?

*Let another man praise you, and not your own
mouth. Let a stranger, and not your own lips.*
PROVERBS 27:2

A humble person acts with respect when he or she wins a game or does anything else to be proud of. Being humble means remembering that God helped you win and thanking Him first. It means thanking all the people who helped you. When you are humble, you let others talk about what you did instead of you telling the world how wonderful you are. It's okay to feel proud and happy when you do something great, but stop and think about how others feel. Make them a part of the celebration instead of wanting all the attention yourself.

HEAVENLY FATHER, THANK YOU FOR HELPING ME DO
GREAT THINGS AND FOR TEACHING ME HOW TO ACT
WHEN I'M FEELING HAPPY AND PROUD. AMEN.

We Are Equally Important

My Christian brothers, our Lord Jesus Christ is the Lord of shining-greatness. Since your trust is in Him, do not look on one person as more important than another.

JAMES 2:1

The New Testament writer James wrote about two men going to church, one dressed in fine clothes, the other in ragged clothes. James said, "What if you show respect to the man in good clothes and say, 'Come and sit in this good place'? But if you say to the poor man, 'Stand up over there'. . .are you not thinking that one is more important than the other?" (James 2:3–4). Jesus doesn't care if we dress in fine clothes or ragged clothes. He sees all of us as equally important—one just as important as another—and that is how He wants us to see one another.

JESUS, HELP ME NEVER TO THINK OF SOMEONE AS LESS IMPORTANT THAN ME. AMEN.

You Don't Understand!

Jesus understands every weakness of ours, because he was tempted in every way that we are. But he did not sin!
HEBREWS 4:15 CEV

Imagine this: You want to do something that's really important to you, but your parents say no. You really, *really* want to do that thing, so you keep asking, and they keep saying no. Finally, you give up and tell them, "You just don't understand!" It's hard when people don't understand your feelings. But remember this: Good feelings or bad Jesus always knows how you feel. If you take time to talk with Him about it, He will help you to feel better. Moms and dads have good reasons for saying no. So try your best to understand that they are doing what they believe is right.

JESUS, THANK YOU FOR UNDERSTANDING MY FEELINGS AND CARING FOR ME ALL THE TIME. AMEN.

Speak Up

Open your mouth. Be right and fair in what you decide. Stand up for the rights of those who are suffering and in need.

PROVERBS 31:9

If you see someone being treated badly, it's easy to walk away and do nothing. But that isn't what Jesus did. He helped. When you see someone being mistreated, the safest thing to do is tell a grown-up. It's good for us to stand up for others and to speak up for what we know is right. Helping one another is how we show love for one another. We are all part of God's big family, and we should think of one another as brothers and sisters. What would you do if you saw someone mistreating your sister or brother?

DEAR GOD, IF I SEE SOMEONE BEING TREATED BADLY, HELP ME TO DO THE RIGHT THING AND TELL SOMEONE. AMEN.

God Created Life

Then God said, "Let the earth bring into being living things after their kind."
GENESIS 1:24

After God created earth, He filled it up with all kinds of living things. People, animals, and plants are living things. But there are other things, very tiny things, that are alive. Bacteria are tiny living things that can get inside our bodies and make us sick. Other tiny things called "cells" in our bodies fight bacteria to help us get well. Every living thing that God created has a purpose and is precious—valuable—in His sight. That is the very best reason to respect everything that is alive. We should do our best to help even the tiniest things stay alive to carry out God's purpose. What is the tiniest living thing you can think of?

DEAR GOD, GUIDE ME TO RESPECT EVERY LIVING THING. AMEN.

We Are Like God

And God made man in His own likeness.
In the likeness of God He made him.
He made both male and female.

GENESIS 1:27

God made us to be like Him. We can never be perfect like God is, but we are like Him because we know what is right and wrong. God lets us choose how to behave. When we try to be like God, we behave in ways that are good. We love others and care about helping them. We are forgiving and fair, and we tell the truth and make wise decisions. God also made us like Him so we would have good ideas and create things. What have you created that you are proud of?

HEAVENLY FATHER, YOU CREATED ME TO BE A LOT LIKE YOU. HELP ME TO FOLLOW YOUR TEACHING AND BEHAVE IN WAYS THAT ARE RIGHT AND GOOD. AMEN.

Quiet, Please

Your beauty should be a gentle and quiet
spirit. In God's sight this is of great worth
and no amount of money can buy it.
1 PETER 3:4

Some kids are quiet. They don't say much, and that might make it hard for them to make friends. God could say those kids have a "quiet spirit." They are just as treasured by Him as you are. If you know a quiet kid, try to be friends. Always be understanding that some kids just need to be quiet sometimes. It's part of who they are, and it's okay. Quiet kids, loud kids, little kids, big kids, kids from every country, kids who look like you and those who don't—all kids are precious in God's sight.

DEAR GOD, PLEASE HELP OTHER PEOPLE
UNDERSTAND THAT SOMETIMES I LIKE BEING
QUIET. IT'S PART OF HOW YOU MADE ME. AMEN.

I Like to Talk

Let the words of my mouth and the thoughts of
my heart be pleasing in Your eyes, O Lord.
PSALM 19:14

Some kids talk a lot. They have something to say about everything. God loves hearing kids' voices, but He wants their words to be good. Every word that comes from someone's mouth should be pleasing to God. Angry words, swear words, words that say bad things about others—those words don't please Him. Instead, we should choose words that are kind, understanding, and make others feel good about themselves. Listen to your words and imagine saying them to God instead of to others. And if you hear yourself talking too much, remember to stop and listen. Give others a chance to say their words.

HEAVENLY FATHER, TEACH ME TO USE WORDS THAT PLEASE YOU, AND ALSO HELP ME TO BE A GOOD LISTENER. AMEN.

God Will Help Me

But Moses said to the Lord, "See, I am not able to speak well. How then will Pharaoh listen to me?"
EXODUS 6:30

The Bible tells us that God wanted a man named Moses to go and speak a message to Pharaoh (a very important leader). Moses worried because he had trouble speaking. Maybe you know someone like him, someone who has trouble saying their words. Moses' problem made him afraid to try. So God gave Moses a helper, someone who would give him the confidence—courage—he needed to do what God wanted. If God wants us to get something done, He will always find a way to help us. Think about this: Has God ever sent you a helper when you were afraid to try?

DEAR GOD, WHEN I NEED A HELPER, I KNOW
I CAN ALWAYS COUNT ON YOU. AMEN.

I Will Help You

That's why you must encourage and help each other, just as you are already doing.
1 THESSALONIANS 5:11 CEV

Some people have problems with their bodies that make them feel shy. Maybe, like Moses, they have trouble saying their words, or maybe they have allergies to certain foods and can't eat what others can. Asthma is something that gets in the way of breathing, and it keeps some people from running and playing sports. If you know someone who has a problem that keeps them from doing things, be understanding and kind. Do your best to help others be less shy and feel good about themselves. God just might be using you as His helper.

GOD, I WANT TO HELP OTHERS TO FEEL GOOD ABOUT THEMSELVES. NO ONE SHOULD BE SHY ABOUT PROBLEMS WITH THEIR BODIES—YOU MADE THEM, AND ALL ARE BEAUTIFUL IN YOUR SIGHT. AMEN.

I Will Help You If. . .

God always does what is right. He will not
forget the work you did to help the Christians
and the work you are still doing to help them.
This shows your love for Christ.

HEBREWS 6:10

When you help others, do you expect something in return? Jesus never said to anyone, "I will help you if you help Me." Jesus helped many people, never asking or expecting anything in return. When you help others without expecting anything from them, God sees what you've done. He won't forget that you were kind and good. When you help others and show them some love, it's as if you are helping and loving God. The Bible says God loves a cheerful giver (see 2 Corinthians 9:7). Be someone who is happy to give some help to anyone in need.

DEAR GOD, I WILL ALWAYS DO MY BEST TO HELP
WITHOUT EXPECTING ANYTHING IN RETURN. AMEN.

You Have Beautiful Hair

"Your flowing hair is like strings of purple.
The king is held by the beauty of your hair."
SONG OF SOLOMON 7:5

Have you seen people with dyed streaks of color in their hair? In the Bible, the Song of Solomon, a young man describes his girlfriend's hair as looking like strings of purple. Even in Bible times, people had their own special hairstyles. Look around you at all the different styles of hair. Some people have thin hair that's long and straight. Others have short, thick, curly hair. People have different hair colors: black, brown, red, blond. Girls sometimes wear clips, ties, or barrettes in their hair. People use different products in their hair too—shampoos, conditioners, gels, and sprays. Whatever kind of hair they have, however they style it—God gave them beautiful hair!

THANK YOU, GOD, FOR MY BEAUTIFUL HAIR. AMEN.

Your Skin Is Beautiful

My skin is dark and beautiful, like a tent
in the desert or like Solomon's curtains.
SONG OF SOLOMON 1:5 CEV

Each crayon in your crayon box has a name—names like peach, melon, cinnamon, black, brown. When you draw, you choose which colors to use. God chose our skin colors when He made us. If you look around you, you'll see many different colors of skin. You might even compare the colors to things you know. Skin can be the color of coconut, a penny, chocolate, licorice, wheat, honey, sand, and everything in between. If you drew a picture of you with all your friends, would you use many different colors? No matter what color skin you are in, God gave you a beautiful color.

DEAR GOD, THANK YOU FOR MY BEAUTIFUL SKIN. AMEN.

Be Careful What You See

"The eye is the light of the body. If your eye is good, your whole body will be full of light. If your eye is bad, your whole body will be dark."
MATTHEW 6:22–23

You learn by seeing how to make things, how things grow, what the world looks like. . . . God wants you to let all those good things inside through your eyes. But He wants you to be careful not to allow bad things to creep in. Video games, television shows, movies, and books can have pictures that don't please God. Stay away from those things, because they can get into your heart where the Holy Spirit lives. Keep your eyes trained on what's right and good. Then what you see will please Him.

HEAVENLY FATHER, HELP ME TO ALLOW ONLY GOOD THINGS
TO COME THROUGH MY EYES TO MY HEART. AMEN.

Animals Can Teach Me

"But ask the wild animals, and they will teach you. Ask the birds of the heavens, and let them tell you."

JOB 12:7

We learn from one another and we learn from God's animals too. Any kind of pet will teach you to be responsible—to make good decisions about its care. A puppy can teach you patience while you help it to learn. Wild animals also teach us. They help us see all the ways God cares for them. He gives animals something called "instinct." It means they know in their hearts what's best to do. People have instinct too. It's that little voice inside you that says, *Uh-oh, I better not do that* or *I better do this!* Get in the habit of watching animals. See what they can teach you.

DEAR GOD, PLEASE SHOW ME WHAT I CAN
LEARN FROM YOUR ANIMALS. AMEN.

Animals Can Be Helpers

*"Who teaches us more than the animals of the earth,
and makes us wiser than the birds of the heavens?"*

JOB 35:11

Just like people, animals are precious in God's sight. Not only does He use them to teach us, but He uses them to help us. Service animals work for people in different ways. Dogs help police officers. They use their noses to find things. Dogs also help blind people by seeing for them and leading the way. Some people take their dogs to hospitals and care centers to cheer up the people there. Different kinds of animals entertain us by doing tricks, and best of all, some cuddle with us and help us feel better when we are sick or sad. What is your favorite animal?

DEAR GOD, I'M GLAD YOU MADE ANIMALS. I LOVE SEEING
ALL THE NEAT THINGS THEY CAN DO. AMEN.

I Can Create Things

You alone are the LORD, Creator of the heavens and all the stars, Creator of the earth and those who live on it, Creator of the ocean and all its creatures.
NEHEMIAH 9:6 CEV

God is the perfect Creator. He can make anything! God wants us to create things too. Everyone is good at making something. What do you like to create? Maybe you like to paint or make music. Do you enjoy baking cookies or other treats? Making up stories and writing them down is another way to be creative. People use their imaginations to make different things in different ways. Some build things, some create art, others sew or make jewelry or crafts. Ask your family and friends what they like to make.

HEAVENLY FATHER, THANK YOU FOR GIVING US DIFFERENT IDEAS FOR THINGS WE CAN MAKE AND DO. AMEN.

We Make Music Together

And all the people went up after him.
They were playing music and were filled with
joy. The earth shook with all the noise.

1 KINGS 1:40

People all around the world speak different languages and live in different ways. But one way all people are alike is that they make music. Everyone everywhere makes music. We can listen to one another's music and enjoy it. The same musical notes are used all over the world. People put them together in different ways to make their own kinds of songs. They sing and use many different instruments to play their music. Some use music to worship and praise God. The Bible says there is music in heaven. Can you imagine how beautiful that music must be?

DEAR GOD, I'M GLAD YOU CREATED MUSIC! I LOVE TO SING AND LISTEN TO MANY DIFFERENT KINDS OF SONGS. AMEN.

Heaven Is My Forever Home

"There are many rooms in My Father's house. . . .
I am going away to make a place for you."
JOHN 14:2

Before Jesus left earth to be with God, He said He was going to make a place for us in heaven. He told us there is plenty of room there for everyone. Heaven is our forever home. When we get there, we will find that it is a perfect and wonderful place. We won't be lonely or alone, because God is there and so will be everyone we know who puts their trust in Jesus. People from all over earth will be there, and they won't speak different languages anymore. We will understand one another. Our bodies will be perfect, and we will all love one another.

DEAR JESUS, I KNOW YOU HAVE A HOME WAITING FOR ME IN HEAVEN. I'LL SEE YOU WHEN I GET THERE. AMEN.

Praise God!

Let's praise God! He listened when
I prayed, and he is always kind.
PSALM 66:20 CEV

Kids all over the world pray to God and praise Him. Praising God means telling Him you think He is wonderful. God is amazing, and there are many reasons to praise Him. God is great because He stays with you all the time. He is everywhere, and He knows all about you. He loves you and cares for you. God sees when you cry, and He comforts you. God always forgives you. Can you think of more reasons to praise Him? Join in with kids all over the world. Say a prayer right now and give God some praise.

DEAR GOD, I THINK YOU ARE AWESOME. YOU ARE SO PERFECT, AND YOU FILL UP MY HEART WITH YOUR LOVE. EVERY DAY YOU GIVE ME MORE REASONS TO PRAISE YOU. AMEN.

God Blesses Me

May you be blessed by the LORD,
Who made heaven and earth.
PSALM 115:15 NKJV

Anything that is good is a blessing. God gives you blessings because He loves you and wants you to have good things. The more you learn about God, the better you understand the ways He blesses you. Blessings can come in little ways, for example, when your grandma surprises you by taking you out for ice cream. Blessings come in bigger ways too. God blesses you with a family, friends, good health, courage, fun. His greatest blessing is Jesus. God gave you Jesus to love you, to learn from, and also to make a way for you to get into heaven one day. God's blessings aren't just for you. He blesses kids and grown-ups everywhere!

HEAVENLY FATHER, YOU ARE SO GOOD TO ME!
THANK YOU FOR YOUR MANY BLESSINGS. AMEN.

I Am a Gift from God

See, children are a gift from the Lord.
The children born to us are our special reward.

PSALM 127:3

You are precious to God. You are also precious to people right here on earth. Your family treasures you. That means they think you are extra-special. You are everything they want and need, one of a kind, and so very loved. Your friends think you are special too, although they might not always say so. You are precious to every person you help. When you are someone's helper, you reward them by giving them what they need. God gave earth a gift when He made you. The world needed you, and God sent you at exactly the right time so every day you could be somebody's special someone.

DEAR GOD, IT FEELS GOOD KNOWING THAT MY FAMILY, FRIENDS, AND OTHERS THINK I'M SPECIAL. AMEN.

Tell Me a Story

"Those who hear the Word of
God and obey it are happy."
LUKE 11:28

The Bible is filled with true stories about real people. You can read about Noah building a huge boat and saving every kind of animal from a great flood. There's the story of a man named Jonah who was swallowed by a gigantic fish that then spit him out alive. And Daniel who was locked in a den with a bunch of ferocious lions, but God kept him safe. In the Bible, you can read about the first Christmas—the day Jesus was born. There's a story about a little boy whose lunch fed five thousand people, and the best story of all about Jesus dying and then coming back to life so that we might also be raised to life and live with Him forever. The Bible is the best book ever written.

DEAR GOD, THANK YOU FOR THE BIBLE. AMEN.

Trust God

Trust in the Lord with all your heart, and do not trust in your own understanding. Agree with Him in all your ways, and He will make your paths straight.
PROVERBS 3:5-6

Sometimes differences get in the way of us getting along. Maybe you've had a disagreement with someone and nothing you did made it better. When you don't know what to do, you can always turn to God. He has the answers to everything. God knows when things aren't going well for you. You can pray and talk with Him about it. You can also look for answers in the Bible. Its words and stories will teach you how to get along better with others. When things aren't going your way, trust God to help. Listen to His Words and follow what they teach you.

DEAR GOD, YOU ARE MY HELP, AND I TRUST YOU. AMEN.

Gather Together

*"Where two or three are gathered together
in My name, there I am with them."*

MATTHEW 18:20

Kids working together make good things happen. There are many ways you and your friends can team up to get things done. You can help keep the earth clean by picking up trash and recycling it. You can help older adults in care centers by visiting with them or making things for them. Kids get together to help donate food and clothing to the poor. They participate in events for special causes. Whatever you do, God will help when you and your friends gather together to get things done. If you notice a problem, talk with your friends about it. See if by working together you can do something to help fix it.

JESUS, SHOW ME WHAT MY FRIENDS AND I CAN DO TOGETHER
TO HELP MAKE THE WORLD A BETTER PLACE. AMEN.

Why Can't We All Just Get Along?

Jesus said to him, "You must love the Lord your God with all your heart and with all your soul and with all your mind."

MATTHEW 22:37

People have always had trouble loving God, and that causes them to have trouble loving and getting along with one another. Jesus said that the greatest of God's laws is to love Him with all our hearts. If we love God so much that we want to be more like Him, it helps us all to love one another. We learn from God to be kind, understanding, helpful, forgiving, and fair. Do your best to put God first and love Him with all your heart. Work at being more like Him and see if it helps you and others to get along.

DEAR GOD, HELP ME TO LOVE YOU EVEN MORE THAN I DO RIGHT NOW. AMEN.

Who Is My Neighbor?

"You must love your neighbor as you love yourself."
MATTHEW 22:39

God's greatest law is "Love the Lord your God with all your heart and with all your soul and with all your mind" (Matthew 22:37). God's second-greatest law is to "love your neighbor as you love yourself." Who are your neighbors? Neighbors aren't just the people next door, across the street, or even in your city or town. Your neighbors are all the people you meet near and far. Whether God puts you together with people with whom you are alike or different, you are to love them. When you love others, it's like God is loving them through you. Think about all the ways you take good care of yourself and do nice things for yourself—those are the ways you should also love others. Be good to yourself. Be kind to others. Spread God's love all around.

HEAVENLY FATHER, PLEASE HELP ME
TO LOVE MY NEIGHBORS. AMEN.

I Am Lovable

Your hands made me and put me together.
PSALM 119:73

Everyone has unhappy days when they don't feel much love. But love isn't all about feelings. Love is more about who you are. The greatest reason to believe you are loved is that you are God's child. God made you, so you are His. When He made you, God thought you were awesome. He still thinks so! Even on your not-so-good days, God loves you. He puts people all around you who love you. Your parents, other family members, and friends love you. Best of all, Jesus loves you! So, on days when you feel a little less lovable, remember this—you are God's child. You are always lovable, always loved, and precious in His sight.

DEAR JESUS, WHEN I FEEL A LITTLE LESS LOVED, HELP ME TO REMEMBER JUST HOW MUCH YOU LOVE ME. AMEN.

Everyone Needs Jesus

I have been chosen to be a missionary and a preacher and a teacher of this Good News.
2 TIMOTHY 1:11

Do you remember the Good News? It's that Jesus loves us and makes a way for us to go to heaven someday. Are you keeping that Good News a secret, or are you sharing it with your family and friends? Everyone needs Jesus. The best gift you can give people is to teach them about Jesus. You should always hope that they will learn to love Him and put their trust in Him. Talk with your friends about Him. Make Jesus a part of your every day. Try this: Gather with your friends to pray and sing worship songs to Jesus. Make up a song about Him together. Then sing your song to others.

DEAR JESUS, LEAD ME TO THOSE WHO
NEED TO KNOW YOU. AMEN.

We Are Delightfully Different

Each kind of seed becomes a different kind of body.
1 CORINTHIANS 15:38

Imagine that someone gives you a pack of different kinds of seeds. You plant them in the same patch of earth, not knowing what each seed will become. The seeds sprout and grow into strong, healthy plants. Then, one day, each plant produces a flower. Together those delightfully different flowers create the loveliest garden you have ever seen. People are somewhat like those flowers. Each person is different—people have different skin, hair, and eye colors; people wear their own styles; people share their special talents by singing, dancing, acting, and making art; people show love and kindness in different ways. Put them all together and what do you have? One big, beautiful world!

DEAR GOD, I'M GLAD YOU MADE US ALL TO BE DIFFERENT. TOGETHER WE ARE BEAUTIFUL! AMEN.

Who Are My Ancestors?

*We have heard them and known them
by what our ancestors have told us.*
PSALM 78:3 NCV

Before you were born, there were your parents, your grandparents, your great-grandparents, their parents, and so on. Your ancestors are the family members who lived on earth before you, some of them so long ago that they were alive when the Bible was written! The lessons children learned from their parents kept being passed down. Today you are learning from your parents some of the same things they learned from their parents. Older people are very wise. God put them in your life to teach you. Ask your grandparents to tell you stories about when they were little. How were their lives different from yours? What good lessons have they learned?

HEAVENLY FATHER, I'M GRATEFUL FOR MY ANCESTORS. I HOPE I WILL MEET THEM IN HEAVEN SOMEDAY. AMEN.

I Will Obey My Parents

Children, as Christians, obey your parents.
This is the right thing to do.

EPHESIANS 6:1

The Bible says parents have the important job of teaching their children to love Jesus. When parents know and love Jesus, they pass down what they know to their children. They teach them to be more like Jesus and do what is right. Do you get angry with your parents when they tell you no? Some lessons about right and wrong take time to learn. You might not always understand if your parents say no to something you want or when they are unhappy with something you do. But be patient with them and obey them. Trust that your parents are teaching you to grow up in a way that pleases God.

DEAR GOD, HELP ME TO OBEY MY PARENTS. THEY ARE TEACHING ME TO BE MORE LIKE JESUS. AMEN.

What Am I Good At?

We all have different gifts that God has given to us by His loving-favor. We are to use them.
ROMANS 12:6

What is something you've never done that you would like to try? Maybe you would enjoy ice skating, gymnastics, playing an instrument, or building something. The Bible says God gives you different gifts—things you do well. Some gifts are hidden. You discover them by sampling many new things. If you find something you're good at, you should work at it to become even better. God gave you your gifts for a purpose, so don't hide them. Share your gifts with others and use them to please God.

DEAR GOD, THERE ARE THINGS I WOULD LIKE TO TRY, BUT SOMETIMES I'M AFRAID. WILL YOU HELP ME? I KNOW THAT WHEN I TRY, I MIGHT FIND SOMETHING I'M REALLY GOOD AT. AMEN.

What Will I Be?

Whatever work you do, do it with all your heart. Do it for the Lord and not for men.
COLOSSIANS 3:23

Have you wondered, *What will I be when I grow up?* God already has that planned. God plans different jobs for everyone. You might be a doctor one day. Your best friend might be an actor. The girl next door could become an architect. God will take some of the things you are good at right now and make them grow. You will want to get better at them, and one day those things will be part of your work. When you get a job someday, you should remember that God led you there. You should do your job as if you are working for Him.

DEAR GOD, I WONDER WHAT YOU HAVE PLANNED
FOR ME. WHAT WILL I BE WHEN I GROW UP? AMEN.

That's Not Fair!

"See, I cry, 'Someone is hurting me!' but I get no answer. I call for help, but no one stands for what is right and fair."

JOB 19:7

People can be mean sometimes and treat others badly. They make fun of them, call them names, and won't include them because they are different. That's not right. Jesus loves all of us, and He wants us to love and be kind to one another. No one should be made fun of because they are different. No one deserves to be called names. We are all God's good creation, and all those who have given their lives to Jesus are sisters and brothers in Christ. So if we see someone being treated badly, we should do what Jesus would: Stand up for them and say, "That's not fair!"

DEAR JESUS, HELP ME TO BE LOVING, KIND, AND FAIR LIKE YOU ARE. AMEN.

Why Do You Do That?

Our Lord Jesus Christ and God our Father loves us.
2 THESSALONIANS 2:16

Liam's family attends church on Saturday. Harper's family eats fish every Friday. The men in Jacob's family wear little black hats on their heads. On Thanksgiving Mia's family enjoys lasagna along with their turkey dinner. Each family is different and does things differently. Different is good. Talking about our differences is how we learn about one another. Always be respectful when you ask someone why they do something. Tell them you are asking because you are interested and you want to get to know them better. Remember that God made us to be different, and He loves us all.

DEAR GOD, I LIKE LEARNING ABOUT THE WAYS WE ARE DIFFERENT. WHEN I ASK OTHERS ABOUT OUR DIFFERENCES, PLEASE HELP ME TO BE RESPECTFUL. GIVE ME THE RIGHT WORDS TO SAY. AMEN.

Old and Young Work Together

They drew names for their work, the young and old alike, also the teacher and the one who was taught.
1 CHRONICLES 25:8

God uses people of all ages. When older and younger people work together, they get things done. Imagine you and your family building a birdhouse together. Your grandpa's job might be designing the house because he's built one before and he knows how to do it. Your dad's job might be cutting wood and putting the birdhouse together. You help with painting. Your younger sister's job is picking the best spot for the house. All ages working together build a fine birdhouse. Can you think of an example of old and young people working together in your own family?

GOD, I LEARN FROM MY OLDER FAMILY MEMBERS,
AND THEY THINK I'M A REALLY GOOD HELPER.
TOGETHER WE GET THINGS DONE. AMEN.

I Love Sweet Words

Pleasing words are like honey. They are sweet to the soul and healing to the bones.

PROVERBS 16:24

The Bible says words can be sweet like honey. When someone says something that makes you feel good inside, it's almost like eating a big piece of birthday cake made just for you! Some sweet words are for you alone, and they make you feel special. Words can make us feel good about ourselves, or they can make us feel angry and sad. When you choose sweet words that make others feel good inside, your words please God. "I love you" are the sweetest words of all. Can you think of others? Always do your best to choose words that are caring and kind.

DEAR GOD, HELP ME TO BE CAREFUL WITH MY WORDS. I WANT WHAT I SAY TO BE PLEASING TO YOU AND TO OTHERS. AMEN.

We All Are Precious to God

I saw many people. . . . They were from every nation and from every family and from every kind of people and from every language. They were standing before [God's] throne and before [Jesus].

REVELATION 7:9

God allowed a man named John to see what would happen in the faraway future. John saw a crowd of people standing in front of God as He sat on His throne. Jesus was there with God. The people were from all over the world and spoke a variety of languages. What John saw reminds us that no matter who we are, where we come from, or what we look like, if we have given our lives to God, trusting that Jesus died on the cross for our sins and rose from the dead, we are part of God's family and precious in His sight.

DEAR GOD, I WANT TO SEE OTHERS AS YOU SEE THEM— NONE BETTER THAN THE OTHER BECAUSE OF THEIR LOOKS OR WHERE THEY COME FROM. AMEN.

I Will Take Care of the Earth

*The heavens are telling of the greatness
of God and the great open spaces above
show the work of His hands.*
PSALM 19:1

God is great! He created a beautiful world for us to live in. But over time, people became careless with the earth. They allowed it to be littered with trash, they cut down forests, and they let the air become polluted with smoke and fumes from factories and vehicles. When they saw what was happening, some decided to work hard to clean up the earth and keep it clean. Earth is God's home for everyone. What are some things you and your family or friends can do together to help clean up God's earth?

GOD, THANK YOU FOR MAKING EARTH A BEAUTIFUL PLACE FOR US TO LIVE. I WILL DO MY BEST TO KEEP IT CLEAN. AMEN.

Jesus Doesn't Change

*Jesus Christ is the same yesterday
and today and forever.*
HEBREWS 13:8

The same Jesus you read about in the Bible is with you today. Jesus said He is with us always. We can believe that because Jesus always tells the truth. He understands us too. When Jesus lived here on earth, He had a human body like ours. He had human feelings, and He understood the feelings that other people had. When He lived here, Jesus taught us about how God wants us to live. That same Jesus is with us now by His Holy Spirit. We can't see Him with our eyes, but His Holy Spirit lives inside our hearts. Jesus is the same now and forever. The ways He loves and cares for us will never change. Jesus loves you, and He is your Helper. He will never leave you.

DEAR JESUS, YOU WILL NEVER CHANGE.
YOU LOVE ME NOW AND FOREVER. AMEN.

Jesus Is a Friend to All

*"For the Son of Man has come
to save that which was lost."*
MATTHEW 18:11

Jesus isn't just a friend to some people. Jesus is a friend to everyone. He looks for those who are left out, the poor, sick, and weak. He wants to spend time with them, love and help them. Jesus is a friend to those who have no friends. Whether they are young or old, rich or poor, Jesus loves them. Jesus wants everyone to know Him. He wants them to follow Him and trust Him so that one day they will live with Him forever in heaven. You will please Jesus if you do your best to be friends with everyone too, no matter where they live, who they are, young or old, rich or poor.

JESUS, I WILL DO MY BEST TO BE
A FRIEND TO EVERYONE. AMEN.

God Made Them All

The Lord said to Samuel, "Do not look at the way
he looks on the outside or how tall he is."

1 SAMUEL 16:7

Animals come in all shapes and sizes. God made them different and interesting to look at. Giraffes have long, lovely necks. Elephants have huge, strong bodies and trunks able to lift just about anything. Rabbits have big feet made for fast running. Can you imagine if all animals looked alike? That wouldn't be any fun. God made people in all shapes and sizes too. He made them beautiful in their own ways. When you notice how people's bodies look on the outside, remember that God made all bodies, and He sees each one as His beautiful creation. And that's how you should see them.

DEAR GOD, THANK YOU FOR MAKING ALL OF US DIFFERENT
AND BEAUTIFUL IN OUR OWN WAYS. AMEN.

I Love You!

Love does not give up. Love is kind. Love is not jealous. . . . Love does not do the wrong thing. Love never thinks of itself. Love does not get angry. Love does not remember the suffering that comes from being hurt by someone.

1 CORINTHIANS 13:4–5

We show others we love them by how we act. The Bible says that love is being patient with others. Love means not wanting what others have. Love isn't selfish; it is all about giving. Love is about doing what is right and helping others with what they need. Love means not getting angry, and if you do get angry, love is apologizing if your anger hurt someone. Love also means forgiving others if they have hurt you. Can you think of more ways to show love?

GOD, HELP ME TO LOVE OTHERS THE WAY YOU LOVE ME. AMEN.

What Is a Role Model?

"Follow My teachings and learn from Me."
MATTHEW 11:29

Have you taught someone to be more like Jesus? You have if your actions taught that person how to behave in ways that are good, right, and pleasing to God. When you teach someone about things like sharing, helpfulness, caring, and forgiveness, you are being a "role model." A role model is someone you look up to, a teacher. A role model sets a good example for others to follow. Jesus is the best role model. He invites us to follow His teachings and learn from Him. Other than Jesus, who are your role models? Which people in your life have taught you to behave well and act in ways that please God?

DEAR JESUS, YOU ARE MY BEST ROLE MODEL. I WANT TO FOLLOW WHAT YOU TEACH AND BECOME MORE LIKE YOU. AMEN.

God Will Lead You

We make our own plans, but the
LORD decides where we will go.
PROVERBS 16:9 CEV

The Bible tells the story of David, a young shepherd boy who loved playing music on his harp. David was very brave. When soldiers were afraid to fight a huge man named Goliath, young David volunteered. With just a slingshot and a stone, he knocked down that giant! God had great plans for David. The boy became King Saul's musician, and later he became king of Israel! As a little boy, David didn't know he would grow up to be a king, but that was God's plan for David. God has a plan for you too. Who knows what great things you will do when you grow up? God knows, and He will lead you there.

DEAR GOD, I TRUST YOU TO LEAD ME
WHERE YOU WANT ME TO GO. AMEN.

We Have Traditions

Keep a strong hold on what we have taught you by what we have said and by what we have written.
2 THESSALONIANS 2:15

Traditions are special things people do the same way year after year. Your ancestors may have passed down traditions from generation to generation. In America many families enjoy the tradition of gathering together for a big turkey dinner on Thanksgiving Day. African Americans and their friends light a candle on each day of a seven-day holiday in December called Kwanzaa. Watching fireworks on Independence Day is another favorite American tradition. Does your family have traditions? All over the world, kids and their families celebrate special days differently. If you know kids who come from other countries, one way to become better friends is to ask about their traditions.

HEAVENLY FATHER, TRADITIONS ARE SO MUCH FUN! THANK YOU FOR THE SPECIAL WAYS FAMILIES CELEBRATE TOGETHER. AMEN.

All Together Now!

We shared together. And we walked
with the people in the house of God.
PSALM 55:14

Summertime means festivals. Festivals are fun, especially because they bring people together. There are many kinds of festivals. Music festivals are great for listening to and learning about different instruments and music styles. Some of the best festivals are those that feature music and traditions from different countries around the world. There are colorful costumes, dancing, and delicious foods to sample. Church festivals are special events where God's people celebrate knowing one another by sharing food, games, and fun. Even in Jesus' time, people enjoyed getting together at festivals and having fun with their families and friends. Isn't it great that God provides us with so many fun things we can do together?

DEAR GOD, THANK YOU FOR FESTIVALS AND
ALL THE FUN TIMES I SHARE TOGETHER WITH
MY FAMILY AND FRIENDS. AMEN.

What a Lovely Rainbow!

[The] light shining around Him looked like the rainbow in the clouds on a day of rain.
EZEKIEL 1:28

Rainbows have seven different colors: red, orange, yellow, green, blue, indigo (a darker blue), and violet. Without different colors, a rainbow would be just one color and not as pretty. Look around you. How many different skin colors do you see? God made us in different colors, and all put together we are lovely. God's rainbow of people isn't only about skin color. He makes us different in many ways. If you can imagine a rainbow made not just of several colors but of billions, that is what we look like to God. Put together we are His amazing work of art. He thinks we are beautiful.

DEAR GOD, WHENEVER I SEE A RAINBOW, I WILL THINK OF ALL THE WORLD'S PEOPLE AND HOW BEAUTIFUL WE ARE TOGETHER. AMEN.

New Friends Are Everywhere

The person who loves the Father
loves His children also.
1 JOHN 5:1

God wants all kids to feel loved and accepted wherever they go. You can help with that. If there's a new kid in your school or at church, be a friend. Help that person to feel comfortable. Ask your parents if you can have a playdate with your new friend. When you see kids being left out, invite them to play with you, and ask your friends to join in. If you see someone being bullied or picked on, be that person's friend. Tell a grown-up what's going on. You and all the world's kids are God's special creation. Treat one another well. You are precious in His sight.

DEAR GOD, THANK YOU FOR SHOWING ME THAT KIDS
ARE ALIKE IN SO MANY DIFFERENT WAYS. AMEN.

Check Out This Exciting Memory Match Game!

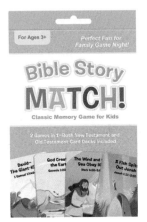

BIBLE STORY MATCH
978-1-64352-279-1 / $12.99

This exciting, "2-games-in-1" Bible memory match is inspired by Old Testament and New Testament Bible story favorites. Deck one features cards with art from Old Testament stories including Noah's Ark, Baby Moses, The Parting of the Red Sea, Strong Man Samson, Jonah and the Whale, and Queen Esther. Deck two includes art from New Testament stories like Jesus Is Born, Fishers of Men, The Woman at the Well, Jesus Walks on Water, The Good Samaritan, The Empty Tomb, and many more!